Man: King
of Mind,
Body, *and*
Circumstance

Man: King *of* Mind, Body, *and* Circumstance

James Allen

Published 2019 by Gildan Media LLC
aka G&D Media
www.GandDmedia.com

Design by Meghan Day Healey of Story Horse, LLC

Library of Congress Cataloging-in-Publication Data is available
upon request

ISBN: 978-1-7225-0238-6

10   9   8   7   6   5   4   3   2   1

Within, around, above, below,
　　The primal forces burn and brood,
Awaiting wisdom's guidance; lo!
　　All their material is good:
Evil subsists in their abuse;
Good, in their wise and lawful use.

Contents

Foreword

The problem of life consists in learning how to live. It is like the problem of addition or subtraction to the schoolboy. When mastered, all difficulty disappears, and the problem has vanished. All the problems of life, whether they be social, political, or religious, subsist in ignorance and wrong-living. As they are solved in the heart of each individual, they will be solved in the mass of men. Humanity at present is in the painful stage of "learning." It is confronted with the difficulties of its own ignorance. As men learn to live rightly, learn to direct their forces and use their functions and faculties by the light of wisdom, the sum of life will be correctly done, and its mastery will put an end to all the "problems of evil." To the wise, all such problems have ceased.

—James Allen
Bryngoleu,
Ilfracombe, England

The Inner World of Thoughts

Man is the maker of happiness and misery. Further, he is the creator and perpetuator of his own happiness and misery. These things are not externally imposed; they are internal conditions. Their cause is neither deity, nor devil, nor circumstance, but Thought. They are the effects of deeds, and deeds are the visible side of thoughts. Fixed attitudes of mind determine courses of conduct, and from courses of conduct come those reactions called *happiness* and *unhappiness*. This being so, it follows that, to alter the reactive condition, one must alter the active thought. To exchange misery for happiness, it is necessary to reverse the fixed attitude of mind and habitual course of conduct which is the cause of misery, and the reverse effect will appear in the mind and life. A man has no power to be happy while thinking and acting selfishly; he cannot be unhappy while thinking and acting unselfishly. Wheresoever the cause is, there the effect will appear. Man cannot abrogate effects, but he can alter causes. He can purify his nature; he can remould his character. There is great power in self-conquest; there is great joy in transforming oneself.

Each man is circumscribed by his own thoughts, but he can gradually extend their circle; he can enlarge and elevate his mental sphere. He can leave the low, and reach up to the high; he can refrain from harbouring thoughts that are dark and hateful, and can cherish thoughts that are bright and beautiful; and as he does this, he will pass into a higher sphere of power and beauty, will become conscious of a more complete and perfect world.

For men live in spheres low or high according to the nature of their thoughts. Their world is as dark and narrow as they conceive it to be, as expansive and glorious as their comprehensive capacity. Everything around them is tinged with the colour of their thoughts.

Consider the man whose mind is suspicious, covetous, envious. How small and mean and drear everything appears to him. Having no grandeur in himself, he sees no grandeur anywhere; being ignoble himself, he is incapable of seeing nobility in any being. Even his god is a covetous being that can be bribed, and he judges all men and women to be just as petty and selfish as he himself is, so that he sees in the most exalted acts of unselfishness only motives that are mean and base.

Consider again the man whose mind is unsuspecting, generous, magnanimous. How wondrous and beautiful is his world. He is conscious of some kind of nobility in all creatures and beings. He sees men as true, and to him they are true. In his presence the meanest forget their nature, and for the moment become like himself, getting a glimpse, albeit confused, in that temporary upliftment, of a higher order of things, of an immeasurably nobler and happier life.

That small-minded man and this large-hearted man live in two different worlds, though they be neighbours. Their consciousness embraces totally different principles. Their actions are each the reverse of the other. Their moral insight is contrary. They each look out upon a different order of things. Their mental spheres are separate, and, like two detached circles, they never mingle. The one is in hell, the other in heaven, as truly as they will ever be, and death will not place a greater gulf between them than already exists. To the one, the world is a den of thieves; to the other, it is the dwelling-place of gods. The one keeps a revolver handy, and is always on his guard against being robbed or cheated (unconscious of the fact that he is all the time robbing and cheating himself), the other keeps ready a banquet for the best. He throws open his doors to talent, beauty, genius, goodness. His friends are of the aristocracy of character. They have become a part of himself. They are in his sphere of thought, his world of consciousness. From his heart pours forth nobility, and it returns to him tenfold in the multitude of those who love him and do him honour.

The natural grades in human society—what are they but spheres of thought, and modes of conduct manifesting those spheres? The proletariat may rail against these divisions, but he will not alter or affect them. There is no artificial remedy for equalizing states of thought having no natural affinity, and separated by the fundamental principles of life. The lawless and the law-abiding are eternally apart, nor is it hatred nor pride that separates them, but states of intelligence and modes of conduct which in the moral principles of things stand mutually unrelated. The rude and ill-mannered are shut out from the circle of the gentle and refined by the impassable wall of their own mentality which, though they may remove by patient self-improvement, they can never scale by a vulgar intrusion. The kingdom of heaven is not taken by violence, but he who conforms to its principles receives the password. The ruffian moves in a society of ruffians; the saint is one of an elect brethren whose communion is divine music. All men are mirrors reflecting according to their own surface. All men, looking at the world of men and things, are looking into a mirror which gives back their own reflection.

Each man moves in the limited or expansive circle of his own thoughts, and all outside that circle is non-existent to him. He only knows that which he has become. The narrower the boundary, the more convinced is the man that there is no further limit, no other circle. The lesser cannot contain the greater, and he has no means of apprehending the larger minds; such knowledge comes only by growth. The man who moves in a widely extended circle of thought knows all the lesser circles from which he has emerged, for in the larger experience all lesser experiences are contained and preserved; and when his circle impinges upon the sphere of perfect manhood, when he is fitting himself for company and communion with them of blameless conduct and profound understanding, then his wisdom will have become sufficient to convince him that there are wider circles still beyond of which he is as yet but dimly conscious, or is entirely ignorant.

Men, like schoolboys, find themselves in standards or classes to which their ignorance or knowledge entitles them. The curriculum of the sixth standard is a mystery to the boy in the first; it is outside and beyond the circle of his comprehension; but he reaches it by persistent effort and patient growth in learning. By mastering and outgrowing all the standards between, he comes at last to the sixth, and makes its learning his own; and beyond still is the sphere of the teacher. So in life, men whose deeds are dark and selfish, full of passion and personal desire, cannot comprehend those whose deeds are bright and unselfish, whose minds are calm, deep, and pure, but they can reach this higher standard, this enlarged consciousness, by effort in right-doing, by growth in thought and moral comprehension. And above and beyond all lower and higher standards stand the Teachers of mankind, the Cosmic Masters, the Saviours of the world whom the adherents of the various religions worship. There are grades in teachers as in pupils, and some there are who have not yet reached the rank and position of *Master*, yet, by the sterling morality of their character, are guides and teachers; but to occupy a pulpit or rostrum does not make a man a teacher. A man is constituted a teacher by virtue of that moral greatness which calls forth the respect and reverence of mankind.

Each man is as low or high, as little or great, as base or noble, as his thoughts; no more, no less. Each moves within the sphere of his own thoughts, and that sphere is his world. In that world in which he forms his habits of thought, he finds his company. He dwells in the region which harmonizes with his particular growth. But he need not perforce remain in the lower worlds. He can lift his thoughts and ascend. He can pass above and beyond into higher realms, into happier habitations. When he chooses and wills he can break the carapace of selfish thought, and breathe the purer airs of a more expansive life.

The Outer World of Things

The world of things is the other half of the world of thoughts. The inner informs the outer. The greater embraces the lesser. Matter is the counterpart of mind. Events are streams of thought. Circumstances are combinations of thought, and the outer conditions and actions of others in which each man is involved are intimately related to his own mental needs and development. Man is a part of his surroundings. He is not separate from his fellows, but is bound closely to them by the peculiar intimacy and interaction of deeds, and by those fundamental laws of thought which are the roots of human society.

One cannot alter external things to suit his passing whims and wishes, but he can set aside his whims and wishes; he can so alter his attitude of mind toward externals that they will assume a different aspect. He cannot mould the actions of others toward him, but he can rightly fashion his actions toward them. He cannot break down the wall of circumstance by which he is surrounded, but he can wisely adapt himself to it, or find the way out into enlarged circumstances by extending his mental horizon. Things follow thoughts. Alter your thoughts, and things will receive a new adjustment. To reflect truly, the mirror must be true. A warped glass gives back an exaggerated image. A disturbed mind gives a distorted reflection of the world. Subdue the mind, organize and tranquilize it, and a more beautiful image of the universe, a more perfect perception of the world-order, will be the result.

Man has all power within the world of his own mind, to purify and perfect it, but his power in the outer world of other minds is subject and limited. This is made plain when we reflect that each finds himself in a world of men and things, a unit amongst myriads of similar units. These units do not act independently and despotically, but responsively and sympathetically. My fellow-men are involved in my actions, and they will deal with them. If what I do be a menace to them, they will adopt protective measures against me. As the human body expels its morbid atoms, so the body politic instinctively expurgates its recalcitrant members. Your wrong acts are so many wounds inflicted on this body politic, and the healing of its wounds will be your pain and sorrow. This ethical cause and effect is not different from that physical cause and effect with which the simplest is acquainted. It is but an extension of the same law; its application to the larger body of humanity. No act is aloof. Your most secret deed is invisibly reported, its good being protected in joy, its evil destroyed in pain. There is a great ethical truth in the old fable of "the Book of Life," in which every thought and deed is recorded and judged. It is because of this—that your deed belongs, not alone to yourself, but to humanity and the universe— that you are powerless to avert external effects, but are all-powerful to modify and correct internal causes; and it is also because of this that the perfecting of one's own deeds is man's highest duty and most sublime accomplishment.

The obverse of this truth—that you are powerless to obviate external things and deeds—is, that external things and deeds are powerless to injure you. The cause of your bondage as of your deliverance is within. The injury that comes to you through others is the rebound of your own deed, the reflex of your own mental attitude. *They* are the instruments, you are the cause. Destiny is ripened deeds. The fruit of life, both bitter and sweet, is received by each man in just measure. The righteous man is free. None can injure him; none can destroy him; none can rob him of his peace. His attitude toward men, born of understanding, disarms their power to wound him. Any injury which they may try to inflict, rebounds upon themselves to their own hurt, leaving him unharmed and untouched. The good that goes from him is his perennial fount of happiness, his eternal source of strength. Its root is serenity, its flower is joy.

The harm which a man sees in the action of another toward him—say, for instance, an act of slander—is not in the act itself, but in his attitude of mind toward it; the injury and unhappiness are created by himself, and subsist in his lack of understanding concerning the nature and power of deeds. He thinks the act can permanently injure or ruin his character, whereas it is utterly void of any such power; the reality being that the deed can only injure or ruin the doer of it. Thinking himself injured, the man becomes agitated and unhappy, and takes great pains to counteract the supposed harm to himself, and these very pains give the slander an appearance of truth, and aid rather than hinder it. All his agitation and unrest is created by his reception of the deed, and not actually by the deed itself. The righteous man has proved this by the fact that the same act has ceased to arouse in him any disturbance. He understands, and therefore ignores it. It belongs to a sphere which he has ceased to inhabit, to a region of consciousness with which he has no longer any affinity. He does not receive the act into himself, the thought of injury to himself being absent. He lives above the mental darkness in which such acts thrive, and they can no more injure or disturb him than a boy can injure or divert the sun by throwing stones at it. It was to emphasize this that Buddha, to the end of his days, never ceased to tell his disciples that so long as the thought "I have been injured," or "I have been cheated," or "I have been insulted," could arise in a man's mind, he had not comprehended the Truth.

And as with the conduct of others, so is it with external things—with surroundings and circumstances—in themselves they are neither good nor bad, it is the mental attitude and state of heart that makes them so. A man imagines he could do great things if he were not hampered by circumstances—by want of money, want of time, want of influence, and want of freedom from family ties. In reality the man is not hindered by these things at all. He, in his mind, ascribes to them a power which they do not possess, and he submits, not to them, but to his opinion about them, that is, to a weak element in his nature. The real "want" that hampers him is the *want of the right attitude of mind.* When he regards his circumstances as spurs to his resources, when he sees that his so-called "drawbacks" are the very steps up which he is to mount successfully to his achievement, then his necessity gives birth to invention, and the "hindrances" are transformed into *aids. The man* is the all-important factor. If his mind be wholesome and rightly tuned, he will not whine and whimper over his circumstances, but will rise up, and outgrow them. He who complains of his circumstances has not yet become a man, and Necessity will continue to prick and lash him till he rises into manhood's strength, and then she will submit to him. Circumstance is a severe taskmaster to the weak, an obedient servant to the strong.

It is not external things, but our thoughts about them, that bind us or set us free. We forge our own chains, build our own dungeons, take ourselves prisoners; or we loose our bonds, build our own palaces, or roam in freedom through all scenes and events. If I think that my surroundings are powerful to bind me, that thought will keep me bound. If I think that, in my thought and life, I can rise above my surroundings, that thought will liberate me. One should ask of his thoughts, "Are they leading to bondage or deliverance?" and he should abandon thoughts that bind, and adopt thoughts that set free.

If we fear our fellow-men, fear opinion, poverty, the withdrawal of friends and influence, then we are bound indeed, and cannot know the inward happiness of the enlightened, the freedom of the just; but if in our thoughts we are pure and free, if we see in life's reactions and reverses nothing to cause us trouble or fear, but everything to aid us in our progress, nothing remains that can prevent us from accomplishing the aims of our life, for then we are free indeed.

Habit: Its Slavery and Its Freedom

an is subject to the law of habit. Is he then free? Yes, he is free. Man did not make life and its laws; they are eternal; he finds himself involved in them, and he can understand and obey them. Man's power does not enable him to make laws of being; it subsists in discrimination and choice. Man does not create one jot of the universal conditions or laws; they are the essential principles of things, and are neither made nor unmade. He discovers, not makes, them. Ignorance of them is at the root of the world's pain. To defy them is folly and bondage. Who is the freer man, the thief who defies the laws of his country, or the honest citizen who obeys them? Who, again, is the freer man, the fool who thinks he can live as he likes, or the wise man who chooses to do only that which is right?

Man is, in the nature of things, a being of habit, and this he cannot alter; but he can alter his habits. He cannot alter the law of his nature, but he can adapt his nature to the law. No man wishes to alter the law of gravitation, but all men adapt themselves to it; they use it by bending to it, not by defying or ignoring it. Men do not run up against walls or jump over precipices in the hope that this law will alter for them. They walk alongside walls, and keep clear of precipices.

Man can no more get outside the law of habit, than he can get outside the law of gravitation, but he can employ it wisely or unwisely. As scientists and inventors master the physical forces and laws by obeying and using them, so wise men master the spiritual forces and laws in the same way. While the bad man is the whipped slave of habit, the good man is its wise director and master. Not its maker, let me reiterate, nor yet its arbitrary commander, but its self-disciplined user, its master by virtue of knowledge grounded on obedience. He is the bad man whose habits of thought and action are bad. He is the good man whose habits of thought and action are good. The bad man becomes the good man by transforming or transmuting his habits. He does not alter the law; he alters himself; he adapts himself to the law. Instead of submitting to selfish indulgences, he obeys moral principles. He becomes the master of the lower by enlisting in the service of the higher. The law of habit remains the same, but he is changed from bad to good by his readjustment to the law.

Habit is *repetition.* Man repeats the same thoughts, the same actions, the same experiences over and over again until they are incorporated with his being, until they are built into his character as part of himself. Faculty is fixed habit. Evolution is mental accumulation. Man, today, is the result of millions of repetitious thoughts and acts. He is not ready-made, he becomes, and is still becoming. His character is predetermined by his own choice. The thought, the act, which he chooses, that, by habit, he becomes.

Thus each man is an accumulation of thoughts and deeds. The characteristics which he manifests instinctively and without effort are lines of thought and action become, by long repetition, automatic; for it is the nature of habit to become, at last, unconscious, to repeat, as it were, itself without any apparent choice or effort on the part of its possessor; and in due time it takes such complete possession of the individual as to appear to render his will powerless to counteract it. This is the case with all habits, whether good or bad; when bad, the man is spoken of as being the "victim" of a bad habit or a vicious mind; when good, he is referred to as having, by nature, a "good disposition."

All men are, and will continue to be, subject to their own habits, whether they be good or bad— that is, subject to their own reiterated and accumulated thoughts and deeds. Knowing this, the wise man chooses to subject himself to good habits, for such service is joy, bliss, and freedom; while to become subject to bad habits is misery, wretchedness, slavery.

This law of habit is beneficent, for while it enables a man to bind himself to the chains of slavish practices, it enables him to become so fixed in good courses as to do them unconsciously, to do instinctively that which is right, without restraint or exertion, and in perfect happiness and freedom. Observing this automatism in life, men have denied the existence of will or freedom on man's part. They speak of him as being "born" good or bad, and regard him as the helpless instrument of blind forces.

It is true that man is the instrument of mental forces—or to be more accurate, he is those forces—but they are not blind, and he can direct them, and redirect them into new channels. In a word, he can take himself in hand and reconstruct his habits; for though it is also true that he is born with a given character, that character is the product of numberless lives during which it has been slowly built up by choice and effort, and in this life it will be considerably modified by new experiences.

No matter how apparently helpless a man has become under the tyranny of a bad habit, or a bad characteristic—and they are essentially the same—he can, so long as sanity remains, break away from it and become free, replacing it by its opposite good habit; and when the good possesses him as the bad formerly did, there will be neither wish nor need to break from that, for its dominance will be perennial happiness, and not perpetual misery.

That which a man has formed within himself, he can break up and re-form when he so wishes and wills; and a man does not wish to abandon a bad habit so long as he regards it as pleasurable. It is when it assumes a painful tyranny over him that he begins to look for a way of escape, and finally abandons the bad for something better.

No man is helplessly bound. The very law by which he has become a self-bound slave will enable him to become a self-emancipated master. To know this, he has but to act upon it—that is, deliberately and strenuously to abandon the old lines of thought and conduct, and diligently fashion new and better lines. That he may not accomplish this in a day, a week, a month, a year, or five years, should not dishearten and dismay him. Time is required for the new repetitions to become established, and the old ones to be broken up; but the law of habit is certain and infallible, and a line of effort patiently pursued and never abandoned, is sure to be crowned with success; for if a bad condition, a mere negation, can become fixed and firm, how much more surely can a good condition, a positive principle, become established and powerful! A man is powerless to overcome the wrong and unhappy elements in himself only *so long as he regards himself as powerless*. If to the bad habit is added the thought, "I cannot," the bad habit will remain. Nothing can be overcome till the thought of powerlessness is uprooted and abolished from the mind. The great stumbling-block is not the habit itself, it is *the belief in the impossibility of overcoming it*. How can a man overcome a bad habit so long as he is convinced that it is impossible? How can a man be prevented from overcoming it when he knows that he can, and is determined to do it? The dominant thought by which man has enslaved himself is the thought, "I cannot overcome my sins." Bring this thought out into the light, in all its nakedness, and it is seen to be a belief in the power of evil, with its other pole, disbelief in the power of good. For a man to say, or believe, that he cannot rise above wrong-thinking and wrong-doing, is to submit to evil, is to abandon and renounce good.

By such thoughts, such beliefs, man binds himself; by their opposite thoughts, opposite beliefs, he sets himself free. A changed attitude of mind changes the character, the habits, the life. Man is his own deliverer. He has brought about his thraldom; he can bring about his emancipation. All through the ages he has looked, and is still looking, for an external deliverer, but he still remains bound. The Great Deliverer is within; He is the Spirit of Truth; and the Spirit of Truth is the Spirit of Good; and he is in the Spirit of Good who dwells habitually in good thoughts and their effects, good actions.

Man is not bound by any power outside his own wrong thoughts, and from these he can set himself free; and foremost, the enslaving thoughts from which he needs to be delivered are—"I cannot rise," "I cannot break away from bad habits," "I cannot alter my nature," "I cannot control and conquer myself," "I cannot cease from sin." All these "cannots" have no existence in the things to which they submit; they exist only in thought.

Such negations are bad thought-habits which need to be eradicated, and in their place should be planted the positive "I can," which should be tended and developed until it becomes a powerful tree of habit, bearing the good and life-giving fruit of right and happy living.

Habit binds us; habit sets us free. Habit is primarily in thought, secondarily in deed. Turn the thought from bad to good, and the deed will immediately follow. Persist in the bad, and it will bind you tighter and tighter; persist in the good, and it will take you into ever-widening spheres of freedom. He who loves his bondage, let him remain bound. He who thirsts for freedom, let him come and be set free.

Bodily Conditions

There are today scores of distinct schools devoted to the healing of the body; a fact which shows the great prevalence of physical suffering, as the hundreds of religions, devoted to the comforting of men's minds, prove the universality of mental suffering. Each of these schools has its place in so far as it is able to relieve suffering, even where it does not eradicate the evil; for with all these schools of healing, the facts of disease and pain remain with us, just as sin and sorrow remain in spite of the many religions.

Disease and pain, like sin and sorrow, are too deep-seated to be removed by palliatives. Our ailments have an ethical cause deeply rooted in the mind. I do not infer by this that physical conditions have no part in disease; they play an important part as *instruments*, as factors in the chain of causation. The microbe that carried the black death was the instrument of uncleanliness, and uncleanliness is, primarily, a moral disorder. Matter is visible mind, and that bodily conflict which we call *disease* has a causal affinity to that mental conflict which is associated with sin. In his present human or self-conscious state, man's mind is continually being disturbed by violently conflicting desires, and his body attacked by morbid elements. He is in a state of mental in harmony and bodily discomfort. Animals in their wild and primitive state are free from disease because they are free from inharmony. They are in accord with their surroundings, have no moral responsibility and no sense of sin, and are free from those violent disturbances of remorse, grief, disappointment, etc., which are so destructive of man's harmony and happiness, and their bodies are not afflicted. As man ascends into the divine or cosmic-conscious state, he will leave behind and below him all these inner conflicts, will overcome sin and all sense of sin, and will dispel remorse and sorrow. Being thus restored to mental harmony, he will become restored to bodily harmony, to wholeness, health.

The body is the image of the mind, and in it are traced the visible features of hidden thoughts. The outer obeys the inner, and the enlightened scientist of the future may be able to trace every bodily disorder to its ethical cause in the mentality.

Mental harmony, or moral wholeness, makes for bodily health. I say *makes for it*, for it will not produce it magically, as it were,—as though one should swallow a bottle of medicine and then be whole and free,—but if the mentality is becoming more poised and restful, if the moral stature is increasing, then a sure foundation of bodily wholeness is being laid, the forces are being conserved and are receiving a better direction and adjustment; and even if perfect health is not gained, the bodily derangement, whatever it be, will have lost its power to undermine the strengthened and uplifted mind.

One who suffers in body will not necessarily at once be cured when he begins to fashion his mind on moral and harmonious principles; indeed, for a time, while the body is bringing to a crisis, and throwing off, the effects of former inharmonies, the morbid condition may appear to be intensified. As a man does not gain perfect peace immediately he enters upon the path of righteousness, but must, except in rare instances, pass through a painful period of adjustment; neither does he, with the same rare exceptions, at once acquire perfect health. Time is required for bodily as well as mental readjustment, and even if health is not reached, it will be approached.

If the mind be made robust, the bodily condition will take a secondary and subordinate place, and will cease to have that primary importance which so many give to it. If a disorder is not cured, the mind can rise above it, and refuse to be subdued by it. One can be happy, strong, and useful in spite of it. The statement so often made by health specialists that a useful and happy life is impossible without bodily health is disproved by the fact that numbers of men who have accomplished the greatest works—men of genius and superior talent in all departments—have been afflicted in their bodies, and today there are plenty of living witnesses to this fact. Sometimes the bodily affliction acts as a stimulus to mental activity, and aids rather than hinders its work. To make a useful and happy life dependent upon health, is to put matter before mind, is to subordinate spirit to body.

Men of robust minds do not dwell upon their bodily condition if it be in any way disordered— *they ignore it*, and work on, live on, as though it were not. This ignoring of the body not only keeps the mind sane and strong, but it is the best resource for curing the body. If we cannot have a perfectly sound body, we can have a healthy mind, and a healthy mind is the best route to a sound body.

A sickly mind is more deplorable than a disordered body, and it leads to sickliness of body. The mental invalid is in a far more pitiable condition than the bodily invalid. There are invalids (every physician knows them) who only need to lift themselves into a strong, unselfish, happy frame of mind to discover that their body is whole and capable.

Sickly thoughts about oneself, about one's body and food, should be abolished by all who are called by the name of *man*. The man who imagines that the wholesome food he is eating is going to injure him, needs to come to bodily vigour by the way of mental strength. To regard one's bodily health and safety as being dependent on a particular kind of food which is absent from nearly every household, is to court petty disorders. The vegetarian who says he dare not eat potatoes, that fruit produces indigestion, that apples give him acidity, that pulses are poison, that he is afraid of green vegetables, and so on, is demoralizing the noble cause which he professes to have espoused, is making it look ridiculous in the eyes of those robust meateaters who live above such sickly fears and morbid self-scrutinies. To imagine that the fruits of the earth, eaten when one is hungry and in need of food, are destructive of health and life is totally to misunderstand the nature and office of food. The office of food is to sustain and preserve the body, not to undermine and destroy it. It is a strange delusion—and one that must react deleteriously upon the body—that possesses so many who are seeking health by the way of diet, the delusion that certain of the simplest, most natural, and purest of viands are *bad of themselves*, that they have in them the elements of death, and not of life. One of these food-reformers once told me that he believed his ailment (as well as the ailments of thousands of others) was caused by eating bread; not by an excess of bread, but by the bread itself; and yet this man's bread food consisted of nutty, homemade, wholemeal loaves. Let us get rid of our sins, our sickly thoughts, our self-indulgences and foolish excesses before attributing our diseases to such innocent causes.

Dwelling upon one's petty troubles and ailments is a manifestation of weakness of character. To so dwell upon them in thought leads to frequent talking about them, and this, in turn, impresses them more vividly upon the mind, which soon becomes demoralized by such petting and pitying. It is as convenient to dwell upon happiness and health as upon misery and disease; as easy to talk about them, and much more pleasant and profitable to do so.

*Let us live happily then, not hating those who
        hate us!*
*Among men who hate us let us dwell free from
        hatred!*

*Let us live happily then, free from ailments
        among the ailing!*
*Among men who are ailing let us dwell free from
        ailments!*

*Let us live happily then, free from greed among
        the greedy!*
*Among men who are greedy let us dwell free
        from greed!*

Moral principles are the soundest foundations for health, as well as for happiness. They are the true regulators of conduct, and they embrace every detail of life. When earnestly espoused and intelligently understood they will compel a man to reorganize his entire life down to the most apparently insignificant detail. While definitely regulating one's diet, they will put an end to squeamishness, food-fear, and foolish whims and groundless opinions as to the harmfulness of foods. When sound moral health has eradicated self-indulgence and self-pity, all natural foods will be seen as they are—nourishers of the body, and not its destroyers.

Thus a consideration of bodily conditions brings us inevitably back to the mind, and to those moral virtues which fortify it with an invincible protection. The morally right are the bodily right. To be continually transposing the details of life from passing views and fancies, without reference to fixed principles, is to flounder in confusion; but to discipline details by moral principles is to see, with enlightened vision, all details in their proper place and order.

For it is given to moral principles alone, in their personal domain, to perceive the moral order. In them alone resides the insight that penetrates to causes, and with them only is the power to at once command all details to their order and place, as the magnet draws and polarizes the filings of steel.

Better even than curing the body is to rise above it; to be its master, and not to be tyrannized over by it; not to abuse it, not to pander to it, never to put its claims before virtue; to discipline and moderate its pleasures, and not to be overcome by its pains—in a word, to live in the poise and strength of the moral powers, this, better than bodily cure, is yet a safe way to cure, and it is a permanent source of mental vigour and spiritual repose.

Poverty

Many of the greatest men through all ages have abandoned riches and adopted poverty to better enable them to accomplish their lofty purposes. Why, then, is poverty regarded as such a terrible evil? Why is it that this poverty, which these great men regard as a blessing, and adopt as a bride, should be looked upon by the bulk of mankind as a scourge and a plague? The answer is plain. In the one case, the poverty is associated with a nobility of mind which not only takes from it all appearance of evil, but which lifts it up and makes it appear good and beautiful, makes it seem more attractive and more to be desired than riches and honour, so much so that, seeing the dignity and happiness of the noble mendicant, thousands imitate him by adopting his mode of life. In the other case, the poverty of our great cities is associated with everything that is mean and repulsive—with swearing, drunkenness, filth, laziness, dishonesty, and crime. What, then, is the primary evil: is it poverty, or is it sin? The answer is inevitable—it is sin. Remove sin from poverty, and its sting is gone; it has ceased to be the gigantic evil that it appeared, and can even be turned to good and noble ends. Confucius held up one of his poor disciples, Yen-hwui by name, as an example of lofty virtue to his richer pupils, yet "although he was so poor that he had to live on rice and water, and had no better shelter than a hovel, he uttered no complaint. Where this poverty would have made other men discontented and miserable, he did not allow his equanimity to be disturbed." Poverty cannot undermine a noble character, but it can set it off to better advantage. The virtues of Yen-hwui shone all the brighter for being set in poverty, like resplendent jewels set in a contrasting background.

It is common with social reformers to regard poverty as the *cause* of the sins with which it is associated; yet the same reformers refer to the immoralities of the rich as being caused by their riches. Where there is a cause its effect will appear, and were affluence the cause of immorality, and poverty the cause of degradation, then every rich man would become immoral and every poor man would come to degradation.

An evil-doer will commit evil under any circumstances, whether he be rich or poor, or midway between the two conditions. A right-doer will do right howsoever he be placed. Extreme circumstances may help to bring out the evil which is already there awaiting its opportunity, but they cannot cause the evil, cannot create it.

Discontent with one's financial condition is not the same as poverty. Many people regard themselves as poor whose income runs into several hundreds, and in some cases several thousands, of pounds a year, combined with light responsibilities. They imagine their affliction to be poverty; their real trouble is covetousness. They are not made unhappy by poverty, but by the thirst for riches. Poverty is more often in the mind than in the purse. So long as a man thirsts for more money he will regard himself as poor, and in that sense he is poor, for covetousness is poverty of mind. A miser may be a millionaire, but he is as poor as when he was penniless.

On the other hand, the trouble with so many who are living in indigence and degradation is that they *are* satisfied with their condition. To be living in dirt, disorder, laziness, and swinish self-indulgence, revelling in foul thoughts, foul words, and unclean surroundings, and to be satisfied with oneself, is deplorable. Here again, "poverty" resolves itself into a mental condition, and its solution, as a "problem," is to be looked for in the improvement of the individual from within, rather than of his outward condition. Let a man be made clean and alert within, and he will no longer be content with dirt and degradation without. Having put his mind in order, he will then put his house in order; indeed, both he and others will know that he has put himself right by the fact that he has put his immediate surroundings right. His altered heart shows in his altered life.

There are, of course, those who are neither self-deceived nor self-degraded, and yet are poor. Many such are satisfied to remain poor. They are contented, industrious, and happy, and desire nothing else; but those among them who are dissatisfied, and are ambitious for better surroundings and greater scope, should, and usually do, use their poverty as a spur to the exercise of their talents and energies. By self-improvement and attention to duty, they can rise into the fuller, more responsible life which they desire.

Devotion to duty is, indeed, not only the way out of that poverty which is regarded as restrictive, it is also the royal road to affluence, influence, and lasting joy, yea, even to perfection itself. When understood in its deepest sense it is seen to be related to all that is best and noblest in life. It includes energy, industry, concentrated attention to the business of one's life, singleness of purpose, courage and faithfulness, determination and self-reliance, and that self-abnegation which is the key to all real greatness. A singularly successful man was once asked, "What is the secret of your success?" and he replied, "Getting up at six o'clock in the morning, and minding my own business." Success, honour, and influence always come to him who diligently attends to the business of his life, and religiously avoids interfering with the duties of others.

It may here be urged—and is usually so urged—that the majority of those who are in poverty—for instance, the mill and factory workers—have not the time or opportunity to give themselves to any special work. This is a mistake. Time and opportunity are always at hand, are with everybody at all times. Those of the poor above mentioned, who are content to remain where they are, can always be diligent in their factory labour, and sober and happy in their homes, but those of them who feel that they could better fill another sphere, can prepare for it by educating themselves in their spare time. The hard-worked poor are, above all, the people who need to economize their time and energies; and the youth who wishes to rise out of such poverty must at the outset put aside the foolish and wasteful indulgences of alcohol, tobacco, sexual vice, late hours at music-halls, clubs, and gaming parties, and must give his evenings to the improvement of his mind in that course of education which is necessary to his advancement. By this method, numbers of the most influential men throughout history—some of them among the greatest—have raised themselves from the commonest poverty; a fact which proves that the time of necessity is the hour of opportunity, and not, as is so often imagined and declared, the destruction of opportunity; that the deeper the poverty, the greater is the incentive to action in those who are dissatisfied with themselves, and are bent upon achievement.

Poverty is an evil or it is not, according to the character and the condition of mind of the one that is in poverty. Wealth is an evil or not, in the same manner, Tolstoi chafed under his wealthy circumstances. To him they were a great evil. He longed for poverty as the covetous long for wealth. Vice, however, is always an evil, for it both degrades the individual who commits it, and is a menace to society. A logical and profound study of poverty will always bring us back to the individual, and to the human heart. When our social reformers condemn vice as they now condemn the rich;

when they are as eager to abolish wrong-living as they now are to abolish low wages, we may look for a diminution in that form of degraded poverty which is one of the dark spots on our civilization. Before such poverty disappears altogether, the human heart will have undergone, during the process of evolution, a radical change. When that heart is purged from covetousness and selfishness; when drunkenness, impurity, indolence, and self-indulgence are driven for ever from the earth, then poverty and riches will be known no more, and every man will perform his duties with a joy so full and deep as is yet (except to the few whose hearts are already pure) unknown to men, and all will eat of the fruit of their labour in sublime self-respect and perfect peace.

Man's Spiritual Dominion

The kingdom over which man is destined to rule with undisputed sway is that of his own mind and life; but this kingdom, as already shown, is not separate from the universe, is not Confined to itself alone; it is intimately related to entire humanity, to nature, to the current of events in which it is, for the time being, involved, and to the vast universe. Thus the mastery of this kingdom embraces the mastery of the knowledge of life; it lifts a man into the supremacy of wisdom, bestowing upon him the gift of insight into human hearts, giving him the power to distinguish between good and evil, also to comprehend that which is above both good and evil, and to know the nature and consequences of deeds.

At present men are more or less under the sway of rebellious thoughts, and the conquest of these is the supreme conquest of life. The unwise think that everything can be mastered but oneself, and they seek for happiness for themselves and others by modifying external things. The transposing of outward effects cannot bring permanent happiness, or bestow wisdom; the patching and coddling of a sin-laden body cannot produce health and well-being. The wise know that there is no real mastery until self is subdued, that when oneself is conquered, the subjugation of externals is finally assured, and they find happiness for ever springing up within them, in the calm strength of divine virtue. They put away sin, and purify and strengthen the body by rising superior to the sway of its passions.

Man can reign over his own mind; can be lord over himself. Until he does so reign, his life is unsatisfactory and imperfect. His spiritual dominion is the empire of the mental forces of which his nature is composed. The body has no causative power. The ruling of the body—that is, of appetite and passion—is the discipline of mental forces. The subduing, modifying, redirecting, and transmuting of the antagonizing spiritual elements within, is the wonderful and mighty work which all men must, sooner or later, undertake. For a long time man regards himself as the slave of external forces, but there comes a day when his spiritual eyes open, and he sees that he has been a slave this long time to none and nothing but his own ungoverned, unpurified self. In that day, he rises up, and, ascending his spiritual throne, he no longer obeys his desires, appetites, and passions as their slave, but henceforth rules them as his subjects. The mental kingdom through which he has been wont to wander as a puling beggar and a whipped serf, he now discovers is his by right of lordly self-control— his to set in order, to organize and harmonize, to abolish its dissensions and painful contradictions, and bring it to a state of peace.

Thus rising up and exercising his rightful spiritual authority, he enters the company of those kingly ones who in all ages have conquered and attained, who have overcome ignorance, darkness, and mental suffering, and have ascended into Truth.

Conquest:
Not Resignation

He who has undertaken the sublime task of overcoming himself, does not resign himself to anything that is evil; he subjects himself only to that which is good. Resignation to evil is the lowest weakness; obedience to good is the highest power. To resign oneself to sin and sorrow, to ignorance and suffering, is to say in effect, "I give up; I am defeated; life is evil, and I submit." Such resignation to evil is the reverse of religion. It is a direct denial of good; it elevates evil to the position of supreme power in the universe. Such submission to evil shows itself in a selfish and sorrowful life; a life alike devoid of strength against temptation, and of that joy and calm which are the manifestation of a mind that is dominated by good.

Man is not framed for perpetual resignation and sorrow, but for final victory and joy. All the spiritual laws of the universe are with the good man, for good preserves and shields. There are no laws of evil. Its nature is destruction and desolation.

The conscious modification of the character away from evil and toward good, forms, at present, no part in the common course of education. Even our religious teachers have lost this knowledge and practice, and cannot, therefore, instruct concerning it. Moral growth is, so far, in the great mass of mankind, unconscious, and is brought about by the stress and struggle of life. The time will come, however, when the conscious formation of character will form an important part in the education of youth, and when no man will be able to fill the position of preacher unless he be a man of habitual self-control, unblemished integrity, and exalted purity, so as to be able to give sound instruction in the making of character, which will then be the main feature of religion.

The doctrine herein set forth by the author is the doctrine of conquest over evil; the annihilation of sin; and necessarily the permanent establishment of man in the knowledge of good, and in the enjoyment of perpetual peace. This is the teaching of the Masters of religion in all ages. Howsoever it may have been disguised and distorted by the unenlightened, it is the doctrine of all the perfect ones that were, and will be the doctrine of all the perfect ones that are to come. It is the doctrine of Truth.

And the conquest is not of an evil without; not of evil men, or evil spirits, or evil things; but of the evil within; of evil thoughts, evil desires, evil deeds; for when every man has destroyed the evil within his own heart, to where in the whole vast universe will any one be able to point, and say, "There is evil"? In that great day when all men have become good within, all traces of evil will have vanished from the earth; sin and sorrow will be unknown; and there will be universal joy for evermore.

James Allen: A Memoir

By Lily L. Allen

from *The Epoch* (February–March 1912)

Unto pure devotion
Devote thyself: with perfect meditation
Comes perfect act, and the right-hearted rise—
More certainly because they seek no gain—
Forth from the bands of body, step by step.
To highest seats of bliss.

James Allen was born in Leicester, England, on November 28th, 1864. His father, at one time a very prosperous manufacturer, was especially fond of "Jim," and before great financial failures overtook him, he would often look at the delicate, refined boy, poring over his books, and would say, "My boy, I'll make a scholar of you."

The Father was a high type of man intellectually, and a great reader, so could appreciate the evident thirst for education and knowledge which he observed in his quiet studious boy.

As a young child he was very delicate and nervous, often suffering untold agony during his school days through the misunderstanding harshness of some of his school teachers, and others with whom he was forced to associate, though he retained always the tenderest memories of others—one or two of his teachers in particular, who no doubt are still living.

He loved to get alone with his books, and many a time he has drawn a vivid picture for me, of the hours he spent with his precious books in his favourite corner by the home fire; his father, whom he dearly loved, in his arm chair opposite also deeply engrossed in his favourite authors. On such evenings he would question his father on some of the profound thoughts that surged through his soul—thoughts he could scarcely form into words—and the father, unable to answer, would gaze at him long over his spectacles, and at last say: "My boy, my boy, you have lived before"—and when the boy eagerly but reverently would suggest an answer to his own question, the father would grow silent and thoughtful, as though he *sensed* the future man and his mission, as he looked at the boy and listened to his words—and many a time he was heard to remark, "Such knowledge comes not in one short life."

There were times when the boy startled those about him into a deep concern for his health, and they would beg him not to *think so much*, and in after years he often smiled when he recalled how his father would say—"Jim, we will have you in the Churchyard soon, if you think so much."

Not that he was by any means unlike other boys where games were concerned. He could play leap-frog and marbles with the best of them, and those who knew him as a man—those who were privileged to meet him at "Bryngoleu"—will remember how he could enter into a game with all his heart. Badminton he delighted in during the summer evenings, or whenever he felt he could.

About three years after our marriage, when our little Nora was about eighteen months old, and he about thirty-three, I realized a great change coming over him, and knew that he was renouncing everything that most men hold dear that he might find Truth, and lead the weary sin-stricken world to Peace. He at that time commenced the practice of rising early in the morning, at times long before daylight, that he might go out on the hills—like One of old—to commune with God, and meditate on Divine things. I do not claim to have understood him fully in those days. The light in which he lived and moved was far too white for my earth-bound eyes to see, and a *sense of it only* was beginning to dawn upon me. But I knew I dare not stay him or hold him back, though at times my woman's heart cried out to do so, waiting him all my own, and not then understanding his divine mission.

Then came his first book, "From Poverty to Power." This book is considered by many his best book. It has passed into many editions, and tens of thousands have been sold all over the world, both authorized and pirated editions, for perhaps no author's works have been more pirated than those of James Allen.

As a private secretary he worked from 9 a.m. to 6 p.m., and used every moment out of office writing his books. Soon after the publication of "From Poverty to Power" came "All These Things Added," and then "As a Man Thinketh," a book perhaps better known and more widely read than any other from his pen.

About this time, too, the "Light of Reason" was founded and he gave up all his time to the work of editing the Magazine, at the same time carrying on a voluminous correspondence with searchers after Truth all over the world. And ever as the years went by he kept straight on, and never once looked back or swerved from the path of holiness. Oh, it was a blessed thing indeed to be the chosen one to walk by the side of his earthly body, and to watch the glory dawning upon him!

He took a keen interest in many scientific subjects, and always eagerly read the latest discovery in astronomy, and he delighted in geology and botany. Among his favourite books I find Shakespeare, Milton, Emerson, Browning, The Bhagavad-Gita, the Tao-Tea-King of Lao-Tze, the Light of Asia, the Gospel of Buddha, Walt Whitman, Dr. Bucke's Cosmic Consciousness, and the Holy Bible.

He might have written on a wide range of subjects had he chosen to do so, and was often asked for articles on many questions outside his particular work, but he refused to comply, consecrating his whole thought and effort to preach the Gospel of Peace.

When physical suffering overtook him he never once complained, but grandly and patiently bore his pain, hiding it from those around him, and only we who knew and loved him so well, and his kind, tender Doctor, knew how greatly he suffered. And yet he stayed not; still he rose before the dawn to meditate, and commune with God; still he sat at his desk and wrote those words of Light and Life which will ring down through the ages, calling men and women from their sins and sorrows to peace and rest.

Always strong in his complete manhood, though small of stature physically, and as gentle as he was strong, no one ever heard an angry word from those kind lips. Those who served him adored him; those who had business dealings with him trusted and honoured him. Ah! how much my heart prompts me to write of his self-sacrificing life, his tender words, his gentle deeds, his knowledge and his wisdom. But why? Surely there is no need, for do not his books speak in words written by his own hand, and will they not speak to generations yet to come?

About Christmas time I saw the change coming, and understood it not—blind! blind! blind! I could not think it possible that *he* should be taken and *I* left.

But we three—as if we knew—clung closer to each other, and loved one another with a greater love—if that were possible—than ever before. Look at his portrait given with the January "Epoch," and reproduced again in this, and you will see that even then our Beloved, our Teacher and Guide, was letting go his hold on the physical. He was leaving us then, and we didn't know it. Often I had urged him to stop work awhile and rest, but he always gave me the same answer, "My darling, when I stop I must go, don't try to stay my hand."

And so he worked on, until that day, Friday, January 12, 1912, when, about one o'clock he sat down in his chair, and looking at me with a great compassion and yearning in those blessed eyes, he cried out, as he stretched out his arms to me, *"Oh, I have finished, I have finished, I can go no further, I have done."*

Need I say that everything that human aid and human skill could do was done to keep him still with us. Of those last few days I dare scarcely write. How could my pen describe them? And when we knew the end was near, with his dear hands upon my head in blessing, he gave his work and his beloved people into my hands, charging me to bless and help them, until I received the call to give up my stewardship!

"I will help you," he said, "and if I can I shall come to you and be with you often."

Words, blessed words of love and comfort, *for my heart alone* often came from his lips, and a sweet smile ever came over the pale calm face when our little Nora came to kiss him and speak loving words to him, while always the gentle voice breathed the tender words to her—*"My little darling!"*

So calmly, peacefully, quietly, he passed from us at the dawn on Wednesday, January 24, 1912. "Passed from us," did I say? Nay, only the outer garment has passed from our mortal vision. He lives! and when the great grief that tears our hearts at the separation is calmed and stilled, I think that we shall know that he is still with us. We shall again rejoice in his companionship and presence.

When his voice was growing faint and low, I heard him whispering, and leaning down to catch the words I heard—"At last, at last—at home—my wanderings are over"—and then, I heard no more, for my heart was breaking within me, and I felt, for *him* indeed it was *"Home at last!"* but for me—And then, as though he knew my thoughts, he turned and again holding out his hands to me, he said: "I have only one thing more to say to you, my beloved, and that is I love you, and I will be waiting for you; good-bye."

I write this memoir for those who love him, for those who will read it with tender loving hearts, and tearful eyes; for those who will not look critically at the way in which I have tried to tell out of my lonely heart this short story of his life and passing away—for *his* pupils, and, therefore, my friends.

We clothed the mortal remains in *pure white linen*, symbol of his fair, pure life, and so, clasping the photo of the one he loved best upon his bosom—they committed all that remained to the funeral pyre.

About the Author

James Allen was one of the pioneering figures of the self-help movement and modern inspirational thought. A philosophical writer and poet, he is best known for his book *As a Man Thinketh*. Writing about complex subjects such as faith, destiny, love, patience, and religion, he had the unique ability to explain them in a way that is simple and easy to comprehend. He often wrote about cause and effect, as well as overcoming sadness, sorrow and grief.

Allen was born in 1864 in Leicester, England into a working-class family. His father travelled alone to America to find work, but was murdered within days of arriving. With the family now facing economic disaster, Allen, at age 15, was forced to leave school and find work to support them.

During stints as a private secretary and stationer, he found that he could showcase his spiritual and social interests in journalism by writing for the magazine *The Herald of the Golden Age.*

In 1901, when he was 37, Allen published his first book, *From Poverty to Power.* In 1902 he began to publish his own spiritual magazine, *The Light of Reason* (which would be retitled *The Epoch* after his death). Each issue contained announcements, an editorial written by Allen on a different subject each month, and many articles, poems, and quotes written by popular authors of the day and even local, unheard of authors.

His third and most famous book *As a Man Thinketh* was published in 1903. The book's minor popularity enabled him to quit his secretarial work and pursue his writing and editing career full time. He wrote 19 books in all, publishing at least one per year while continuing to publish his magazine, until his death. Allen wrote when he had a message—one that he had lived out in his own life and knew that it was good.

In 1905, Allen organized his magazine subscribers into groups (called "The Brotherhood") that would meet regularly and reported on their meetings each month in the magazine. Allen and his wife, Lily Louisa Oram, whom he had married in 1895, would often travel to these group meetings to give speeches and read articles. Some of Allen's favorite writings, and those he quoted often, include the works of Shakespeare, Milton, Emerson, the Bible, Buddha, Whitman, Trine, and Lao-Tze.

Allen died in 1912 at the age of 47. Following his death, Lily, with the help of their daughter, Nora took over the editing of *The Light of Reason*, now under the name *The Epoch*. Lily continued to publish the magazine until her failing eyesight prevented her from doing so. Lily's life was devoted to spreading the works of her husband until her death at age 84.